KT-424-339

CONTENTS

BATMAN'S BUTLER

VITAL STATS

LIKES: Neatness and order
DISLIKES: Reckless behaviour
FRIENDS: Batman and Robin
FOES: The Penguin, Mr Freeze
SKILLS: Acting, medicine
GEAR: None

SET NAMES: The Batcave: The Penguin and Mr Freeze's Invasion
SET NUMBERS: 7783
YEARS: 2006

Bald head accompanies wise expression

Classic LEGO® goblet for taking refreshment to Batman

Alfred's suit rivals those of the Penguin's!

SOME ICE, SIR?

Alfred rarely battles bad guys, but when the Batcave is attacked, he doesn't lose his cool. In fact, he seems positively chilled when Mr Freeze traps him in a block of ice!

Alfred Pennyworth is one of the few people trusted with Batman's biggest secret: his other identity as Bruce Wayne! He provides loyal service at Wayne Manor – and beneath it in the Batcave.

DC COMICS
SUPER HEROES

BAT_____DS

WRITTEN ____ SCOTT

BATMAN ____GER

INTRODUCTION

Whether on the police force, like Commissioner Gordon, or part of the wider super hero community, like Batgirl, Batman's friends are always eager to help him fight crime.

HOW TO USE THIS BOOK

This book is a guide to Batman's super friends and amazing allies. These amazing minifigures are ordered chronologically according to when they were first released.

ROBIN
TRUSTED SIDEKICK

VITAL STATS

LIKES: Working things out
DISLIKES: Unsolved puzzles
FRIENDS: Batman, Alfred, Nightwing
FOES: The Penguin, Mr Freeze
SKILLS: Deduction, swimming
GEAR: Scuba jet

SET NAMES: Robin's Scuba Jet: Attack of The Penguin
SET NUMBERS: 7885
YEARS: 2008

Both 2006 and 2008 Robin minifigures variants wear the same outfit with a bright yellow cape.

Flat hairpiece has also appeared in LEGO® Pharaoh's Quest and LEGO® City sets.

"R" on chest is a stylized throwing star

BIRD ON THE WATER

The Boy Wonder made a splash with a different hairstyle when he sped into battle on his jet ski in The Batcave: The Penguin and Mr Freeze's Invasion (set 7783) in 2006.

When Tim Drake realised that Batman needed help, he used his detective skills to work out the Caped Crusader's secret identity. Batman was so impressed with Tim's abilities that he trained him to become his sidekick – Robin.

SCUBA JET
WONDER GOES UNDER

VITAL STATS

OWNED BY: Robin
USED FOR: Deep-water diving
GEAR: Breathable atmosphere, rocket launchers

SET NAMES: Robin's Scuba Jet: Attack of The Penguin
SET NUMBERS: 7885
YEARS: 2008

Colour scheme with "R" symbols matches Robin's costume

BIRD STRIKE

Robin knows when he's close to the Penguin's Submarine – that's when the Penguin sends his robot helpers to attack. These robo-penguins work just as well under water as on land!

Blaster weapons designed to work underwater

Large, clear canopy gives Robin a wide sea-view

These green engines do not appear in any other LEGO set.

Robin can breathe easy as he dives deep in pursuit of the Penguin. His Scuba Jet has its own air supply so he can stay underwater for extended periods – although its twin turbine engines should bring any chase to a speedy end.

NIGHTWING
SOLO FLYER

VITAL STATS

LIKES: Acrobatics
DISLIKES: Being told what to do
FRIENDS: Batman
FOES: Poison Ivy
SKILLS: Martial arts
GEAR: Escrima sticks

SET NAMES: Arkham Asylum
SET NUMBERS: 7785
YEARS: 2006

Rubber hairpiece created for LEGO® EXO-FORCE™ theme in 2006

Mask shaped like wings spread in flight

Blue and black costume also echoes the wingspan of a bird or a dragon

NIGHT RIDER

Nightwing rides this streamlined cycle to help Batman foil an escape from Arkham Asylum (set 7785). It has space for his two martial arts fighting sticks, also known as escrima, at the back.

Dick Grayson was the first Robin, fighting crime alongside Batman. As he grew older, he wanted to go his own way. He chose Nightwing as his new identity after Superman told him about a legendary Kryptonian character with the same name.

ROBIN
OLDER BOY WONDER

VITAL STATS

LIKES: Using his brains
DISLIKES: Being treated like a kid
FRIENDS: Batman
FOES: The Joker
SKILLS: Detecting
GEAR: Grappling hook

SET NAMES: The Dynamic Duo Funhouse Escape, The Batcave, Robin and the Redbird Cycle
SET NUMBERS: 6857, 6860, 30166
YEARS: 2012, 2012, 2013

DID YOU KNOW?
Several people have fought crime in the guise of Robin, including Dick Grayson, Tim Drake and Damian Wayne.

Robin's head swivels to reveal a shocked expression for when facing the scariest of villains.

Fabric cape similar to Batman's

Utility Belt pouches hold everything a top sidekick needs!

BOY GENIUS AT WORK
Tim Drake is known as the Boy Wonder for a reason! He is a first-class scientist and engineer, and he can use the Batcomputer as well as Batman himself – maybe even better!

Stepping out on his own, but still fighting crime as Robin, Tim Drake dons a more serious, all-red costume. The single colour makes it look like Tim no longer has time for fun, and certainly this variant does not feature a smiling expression.

GUARD
BRAVE BANK EMPLOYEE

VITAL STATS

LIKES: Standing guard
DISLIKES: Bank robbers
FRIENDS: Batman
FOES: Two-Face, henchmen
SKILLS: Brave and resourceful
GEAR: Walkie-talkie, handcuffs

SET NAMES: The Batmobile and The Two-Face Chase, Batman: Arkham Asylum Breakout
SET NUMBERS: 6860, 10937
YEARS: 2012, 2013

The Guard has the same face as the original 2006 Bruce Wayne minifigure.

LEGO handcuffs have appeared in more than 80 sets.

EMPLOYEE OF THE YEAR

Because of his brave actions at the Bank, the guard was offered a job at Arkham Asylum. Keeping a bunch of criminals in their cells? All in a day's work!

Guard uniform printing on torso

ARKHAM ASYLUM

Most bank employees turned and ran when Two-Face raided Gotham City bank. Not this guard. He raised the alarm and called Batman personally, standing ready to handcuff Harvey Dent and his heinous henchmen.

VITAL STATS

LIKES: Caged criminals
DISLIKES: Prison breakouts
FRIENDS: Batman
FOES: The Arkham
Asylum inmates
SKILLS: Recapturing criminals
GEAR: Kendo stick

SET NAME: Batman: Arkham
Asylum Breakout
SET NUMBER: 10937
YEAR: 2013

DID YOU KNOW?

This minifigure is incredibly similar to the Robin in the *Batman: Arkham City* video game.

Hood to hide in the shadows

Two-sided head features a scared expression on the reverse

Shorter cape worn for first time

Black gloves

BETTER THAN A BROLLY

The Penguin better watch out – Robin is armed and dangerous. The monocle-wearing menace may have more than a few tricks up his umbrella, but they're no match for Robin's kendo stick!

When Batman and Robin's greatest enemies escaped Arkham Asylum, the Boy Wonder began the long task of bringing them all back to justice. This hooded variant swapped Robin's usual red legs for black to remain hidden for longer!

ARKHAM VAN

ALL ABOARD FOR ARKHAM

VITAL STATS

OWNER: Arkham Asylum
USED FOR: Prisoner transport
GEAR: Grill guard

SET NAME: Batman: Arkham Asylum Breakout
SET NUMBER: 10937
YEAR: 2012

Blue lights for use in an emergency

Room for one security guard

Arkham and Gotham City logos

Protective grill guard

28MB89

IN THE BACK
Double doors at the back of the van are wide enough to take in a lying-down Joker, his restraining frame and his broad, maniacal grin. He couldn't possibly escape. Could he?

This armoured vehicle serves as a prisoner transport for the most dangerous inmates of Arkham Asylum. The logo on the side lets citizens know they should steer clear, while blue lights on top flash as it speeds through the city!

[COMMISSIONER GORDON]
CHIEF OF GOTHAM CITY POLICE

VITAL STATS

LIKES: Law and order
DISLIKES: Crime and deceit
FRIENDS: Batman
FOES: Bane
SKILLS: Keeping the peace
GEAR: Police handgun

SET NAME: The Bat vs Bane:
Tumbler Chase
SET NUMBER: 76001
YEAR: 2013

Being a cop in
Gotham City
is a scary job!

SWAT stands for
Special Weapons
Attack Team.

Police issue
firearm

SWAT'S GOING ON?
Gordon may look scared but a
twist of his head reveals a calm,
determined face. Years of being
the Gotham City chief of police
have taken their toll. Just look
at those bags under Jim's eyes!

Can a bullet-proof
vest *really* protect
Gordon from
villains like Bane?

Unlike most of the Gotham City
police force, James Gordon is an
honest cop. While Jim doesn't always
approve of Batman's methods,
he realises that the Dark Knight
is Gotham City's last hope against
dangerous super-villains like Bane.

THE BAT
ARMED AND DANGEROUS

VITAL STATS

OWNER: Batman
USED FOR: Aerial pursuit
GEAR: Missiles, rescue rope

SET NAME: The Bat vs Bane: Tumbler Chase
SET NUMBER: 76001
YEAR: 2013

Click-joints allow the "arms" to stay in different positions

Flick-fire missiles on both arms

"Dark Knight"-style bat-symbol

Gordon holds on to the rescue rope

ROOM FOR ONE MORE
The Bat has a second seat in the cockpit so that Gordon can fit behind Batman when he's finished hanging around. Propellers ensure the pair can speed away from Bane.

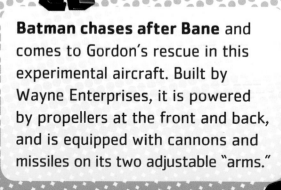

Batman chases after Bane and comes to Gordon's rescue in this experimental aircraft. Built by Wayne Enterprises, it is powered by propellers at the front and back, and is equipped with cannons and missiles on its two adjustable "arms."

VITAL STATS

LIKES: Pranks, the Justice League
DISLIKES: Being overstretched
FRIENDS: Batman
FOES: The Dart
SKILLS: Stretching into any shape he wishes .
GEAR: Groovy goggles

SET NAME: Plastic Man (polybag)
SET NUMBER: 5004081
YEAR: 2014

Plastic Man shares a hairpiece with Superman.

Those goggles make Plastic Man one cool dude – or so he thinks!

A QUICK CHANGE

Plastic Man's costume is also printed on the back. The outfit was inspired by Plastic Man's updated appearance in the 2011 Flashpoint event. This was Plastic Man's first appearance with tights, instead of bare legs.

Boots printed on legs

Given away at U.S. GameStop stores with pre-orders of LEGO *Batman 3: Beyond Gotham*, this exclusive minifigure gave super-stretchy Patrick "Eel" O'Brian a fantastic plastic form. Plastic Man has the power to reshape his body.

14

VITAL STATS

LIKES: Flying
DISLIKES: Explosives
FRIENDS: Batman
FOES: Man-Bat
SKILLS: Fighting, acrobatic circus tricks
GEAR: Grappling hook glider

SET NAMES: Batman: Man-Bat Attack
SET NUMBERS: 76011
YEARS: 2014

DID YOU KNOW?
Nightwing's new black and red costume first appeared in the DC Comics in 2013.

Double-sided head shows expressions of smiling or grim concentration.

Black gloves protect hands when using glider

The "V" of Nightwing's insignia continues on the back of his top.

WINGED WONDER
Just like his mentor, Batman, Nightwing has plenty of cool vehicles. His rocket glider allows him to patrol the skies of Gotham City, keeping an eagle-eye out for trouble.

Acrobatic Dick Grayson enjoys the freedom of fighting crime on his own under the more grown-up identity of Nightwing. As a possible nod to the fact that he was once Robin, he changes his costume from blue to black and red. Neat!

THE ALIEN KNIGHT

VITAL STATS

LIKES: Bright colours
DISLIKES: Shaving
FRIENDS: Batman
FOES: The criminals
of Zur-En-Arrh
SKILLS: Hand-to-hand
fighting
GEAR: Baseball bat

SET NAME: Batman of
Zur-En-Arrh
SET NUMBER: SDCC036
YEAR: 2014

DID YOU KNOW?

This version of the
Caped Crusader first
appeared in a 1940
Batman story called
*The Superman of
Planet X.*

Purple cowl

Two-sided face
with stubble and
growl on one
side and smile
on the other

Plain purple
cape

EXTRA-SPECIAL
EXTRA-TERRESTRIAL

The alien Batman's garish
colours continue on the
minifigure's back. You can also
see his yellow Utility Belt
complete with pockets and
Tiano's radio, capable of
scrambling security systems.

Alien scientist Tiano spent years
monitoring Earth. Impressed by
Batman, Tiano became a cowled
Caped Crusader for his home planet,
Zur-En-Arrh. This colourful
minifigure was an exclusive Comic-
Con release.

VITAL STATS

LIKES: Staying up late
DISLIKES: School nights
FRIENDS: Batman
FOES: Too many to mention
SKILLS: Acrobatics
GEAR: Grappling hook

SET NAMES: Batman Classic TV Series *Batmobile*, Batman: Defend the Batcave
SET NUMBERS: SDCC037, 10672
YEAR: 2014

Wide open yell

Unique head only available on this minifigure

Shorter yellow cape

Green legs adjoin separate red hip piece

JUNIOR CRIME FIGHTER

Although this Boy Wonder was included as a San Diego Comic-Con exclusive, his true home is in this LEGO® Juniors set. Here he can be found working at his Robin-coloured computer and leaping cheerfully off a building to come to Batman's aid!

Fresh-faced and sporting a look inspired by the 1960s *Batman* TV series, Dick Grayson is back in his classic Robin costume. In a style similar to his original 2006 and 2008 variants, Robin once again wears bright primary colours.

ROBIN
THE SON OF BATMAN

VITAL STATS

LIKES: Getting the job done
DISLIKES: The other Robins
FRIENDS: His dad, sometimes
FOES: The Joker, the Joker's Goon
SKILLS: Fighting
GEAR: Quarterstaff

SET NAME: Batman: The Joker Steamroller
SET NUMBER: 76013
YEAR: 2014

Cross expression

Robin's shorter cape looks long on smaller Damian.

Short legs

THE BRAT WONDER

Damian is small but has plenty of attitude. He immediately redesigned the Robin costume and insignia. But, as his alternate face shows, he's often shocked when his father puts him in his place.

Damian is the son of Bruce Wayne. Brought up by his assassin mother, Damian is a skilled, but extremely spoilt, child. On arriving in Gotham City he demanded that he take on the role of Robin. Tim Drake reluctantly stood aside.

BATGIRL
THE COMMISSIONER'S DAUGHTER

VITAL STATS
....

LIKES: Being part of a team
DISLIKES: Being ignored
FRIENDS: Batman, Robin
FOES: The Joker, the
Joker's Goon
SKILLS: Acrobatic tricks
GEAR: Batarang

SET NAME: Batman:
The Joker Steamroller
SET NUMBER: 76013
YEAR: 2014

Double-sided head showing a smile and a frown

Cowl comes complete with red hair

Bright purple cape similar in design to Batman's cape

GIRL POWER
At first Batman wasn't sure about Batgirl. But she soon proved her worth in fights with Gotham City's underworld – from the Joker's henchman to the Clown Prince of Crime himself. In a fight, her trusty Batarang is always by her side!

Torso printing displays a cheerful yellow bat-symbol

Commissioner Gordon's daughter Barbara had always been a Batman fan. She soon follows in the Dark Knight's footsteps, but she has to work hard to keep her identity secret from her detective dad.

SCUBA ROBIN
SUBMARINE SIDEKICK

VITAL STATS

LIKES: Scuba diving
DISLIKES: Chains
FRIENDS: Batman, Aquaman
FOES: Black Manta
SKILLS: Calling for help
GEAR: Handcuffs

SET NAME: Black Manta
Deep Sea Strike
SET NUMBER: 76027
YEAR: 2015

Under the goggles, this side of Robin's face reveals printed-on scuba gear.

Yellow air-tank attached around neck

DID YOU KNOW?
This minifigure also comes with a black hairpiece for when you remove Robin's helmet.

UNDERWATER PRISON
No wonder a twist of Robin's head reveals a scared expression. Not only does Black Manta slap-on the handcuffs, he also attaches a chain to Robin's legs to anchor him to the seabed.

Flippers attach directly to feet

Robin was enjoying a quick dip beneath the waves when Black Manta clapped him in chains and whisked him away in his sinister Sea Saucer. Robin's crime-fighting career has never sunk so low, but he is at least dressed for the occasion.

VITAL STATS

LIKES: Acting alone
DISLIKES: Not being the captain of the ship
FRIENDS: Batman
FOES: Deathstroke
SKILLS: Piloting hover boats
GEAR: Cape

SET NAME: Batboat Harbour Pursuit
SET NUMBER: 76034
YEAR: 2015

DID YOU KNOW?
This minifigure reuses the Robin headpiece from Batman: The Joker Steam Roller (set 76013).

Longer hair

New body armour is more hi-tech

RADAR ROBIN
There was nowhere to hide for Deathstroke as Batman and Robin took to the Batboat. Robin skillfully used the Bat-radar to track down the menacing mercenary.

Dick Grayson may be moving on to fight crime as Nightwing, but he still reappears as Robin every now and again. He can't wait for Batman to let him pilot the Batboat for himself and wears this darker suit in a fight against Deathstroke.

ALFRED
FAITHFUL FRIEND

VITAL STATS
....

LIKES: Dusting and polishing
DISLIKES: Home invasions
FRIENDS: Bruce Wayne,
Dick Grayson
FOES: The Joker
SKILLS: Excellent telephone
manner
GEAR: None

SET NAMES: *Batman* Classic
TV Series – Batcave
SET NUMBERS: 76052
YEARS: 2016

White handkerchief
in breast pocket

Batphone for receiving calls
from Commissioner Gordon

YOU RANG, SIR?
Alfred's daily duties include
answering the Batphone. He
summons Batman if he is at
home, and takes messages from
Commissioner Gordon if the
Caped Crusader is out.

BRUCE

The stately butler of Wayne
Manor, Alfred does much more than
just answer the Batphone. He is a
mechanic, a swordsman and an
archer, and has years of wisdom to
offer the Dynamic Duo. Batman and
Robin would be lost without him!

THE BOY WONDER
WARD OF WAYNE MANOR

VITAL STATS

LIKES: Secretly being Robin
DISLIKES: Writing essays
FRIENDS: Bruce Wayne, Alfred
FOES: Catwoman
SKILLS: Tuba playing, bird calls
GEAR: None

SET NAMES: *Batman* Classic TV Series – Batcave
SET NUMBERS: 76052
YEARS: 2016

Dick models his neat hair after Bruce Wayne's.

Sensible red jumper over white shirt

Smart blue trousers

BATCAVE OR BUST

When duty calls, Dick flips up the bust of Shakespeare on Bruce's desk to reveal a hidden button. Pressing it opens up a secret entrance to the Batcave!

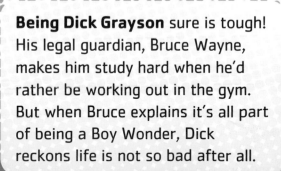

Being Dick Grayson sure is tough! His legal guardian, Bruce Wayne, makes him study hard when he'd rather be working out in the gym. But when Bruce explains it's all part of being a Boy Wonder, Dick reckons life is not so bad after all.

NEW BATCAVE
March 2016 saw the release of a very special LEGO Batcave (set 76052) – in honour of the 1960s *Batman* TV series.

ROBIN
BRIGHT AND BREEZY

VITAL STATS
....

LIKES: Riding in the Batmobile
DISLIKES: Not getting to drive the Batmobile
FRIENDS: Batman, Alfred
FOES: Catwoman, the Joker, the Penguin, the Riddler
SKILLS: Honesty, courage
GEAR: Handcuffs

SET NAMES: *Batman* Classic TV Series – Batcave
SET NUMBERS: 76052
YEARS: 2016

Reverse of head shows alarmed face

Tunic laces up at front

Flesh-coloured tights protect legs

TO THE BATPOLES!
Quick-change Batpoles in the Batcave allow Bruce Wayne and Dick Grayson to become Batman and Robin at the flick of a switch on their way down to the Batmobile.

This colourful sidekick needs an equally colourful oufit. Clad in a smart red tunic and very short green shorts, Robin is ready to save the day in style. That's what makes him Batman's best chum and a vital part of the Dynamic Duo!

SMALL WONDER

VITAL STATS
....
LIKES: Scaling new heights
DISLIKES: Being grounded
FRIENDS: Mighty Micros: Batman
FOES: Mighty Micros: Bane
SKILLS: Climbing, acrobatics
GEAR: Grapple gun

SET NAMES: Mighty Micros: Bane vs Robin
SET NUMBERS: 76062
YEARS: 2016

Same neat hair as red-suited Robin

Mask doesn't hide Robin's happy eyes!

Shorter cape than most Robin minifigures

RELIANT ROBIN
Robin can rely on his Mighty Micros car to get him around on the ground, but he also carries a grapple gun, in case there are any walls to climb!

Non-posable legs

There's nothing at all micro about the smile on this Robin's face! The larger-than-life character couldn't be happier to have his own car for the first time, and he's going to use it to stop Mighty Micros: Bane from causing big trouble in Gotham City!

Project Editor Emma Grange
Editors Tina Jindal, Matt Jones, Ellie Barton,
Clare Millar, Rosie Peet
Senior Designers Nathan Martin, Mark Penfound,
David McDonald
Designers Karan Chaudhary, Stefan Georgiou
Pre-Production Producer Kavita Varma
Senior Producer Lloyd Robertson
Managing Editors Paula Regan,
Chitra Subramanyam
Design Managers Neha Ahuja, Guy Harvey
Creative Manager Sarah Harland
Art Director Lisa Lanzarini
Publisher Julie Ferris
Publishing Director Simon Beecroft
Additional Photography Markos Chouris,
Christopher Chouris, Gary Ombler

First published in Great Britain in 2016
by Dorling Kindersley Limited
80 Strand, London, WC2R 0RL

001–298875–Jul/16

Contains content previously published in LEGO® DC COMICS
SUPER HEROES *Character Encyclopedia* (2016)

Page design copyright © 2016 Dorling Kindersley Limited
A Penguin Random House Company

A CIP catalogue record for this book
is available from the British Library.

ISBN: 978-0-2412-9284-6

Printed and bound in China

www.LEGO.com
www.dk.com

A WORLD OF IDEAS:
SEE ALL THERE IS TO KNOW

ACKNOWLEDGEMENTS

DK would like to thank Randi Sørensen,
Paul Hansford, Martin Leighton Lindhardt, Maria
Bloksgaard Markussen, Adam Corbally, Daniel
Mckenna, Casper Glahder, Adam Siegmund Grabowski,
John Cuppage, Justin Ramsden, Karl Oskar Jonas
Norlen, Marcos Bessa, Sally Aston, Sven Robin Kahl
and Mauricio Bedolla at the LEGO Group; Ben Harper,
Thomas Zellers and Melanie Swartz at Warner Bros.;
Cavan Scott and Simon Hugo for their writing;
Katie Bowden for editorial assistance and Sam
Bartlett for design assistance.